My First
CHAMORRO
200 Picture Word Book
with English translations

GERÅRD AFLÅGUE COLLECTION

Designed by
Gerard Aflague

Translated by
Fermina Sablan

Published by the
GERÅRD AFLÅGUE COLLECTION
Copyright 2017

Foreword

We love investing in our children by designing books
to help them learn the Chamorro language.

Our goal is to invigorate curious and maleable minds of young ones
through language and imagery. It is our desire to instill the complexity of the
language of the Chamorro people and inspire others to embrace a language in a
whole new way.

It is our hope that you will share this book with your friends and family to
spread your love for, and perpetuate the Chamorro culture.

CHAMORRO
PRONUNCIATION
GUIDE

Several Chamorro letters are pronounced differently from English. Use the following guide to help you pronounce words correctly.

å sounds like "au" as in Australia
chålek [chau-lik] /laugh

a sounds like "a" as in fan
chalan [cha-lahn] /road

e sounds like "eh" as in echo
kek [keh-k] /cake

i sounds like "ee" as in knee
nina'i [nee-nah-ee] / gift

o sounds like "oh" as in oreo
boti [boh-tee] / boat

u sounds like "uh" as in rude
ulo' [uh-luh] /worm

y sounds like "dz" as in Yona
yori [dzo-rhee] / flip flop

ch sounds like "ch" as in chime
chagi [chah-gee] / try

j sounds like "h" as in hat
Borja [bor-ha] / Borja (Surname)

ñ sounds like "ny" as in banya
ñamu [nya-mu] mosquito

b sounds like "b" in boy

d sounds like "d" in dog

f sounds like "f" in funny

g sounds like "g" in guy

h sounds like "h" in hat

k sounds like "k" in kick

l sounds like "l" in love

m sounds like "m" in man

n sounds like "n" in never

p sounds like "p" in pad

r sounds like "r" in race

s sounds like "s" in sun

t sounds like "t" in toy

cake
kek

gift
nina'i

coconut tree
trongkon niyok

canoe
la'yak

basketball
basketbo'

apple
mansåna

key
yabi

fish
guihan

car
kareta

toothbrush
guesgues nifin

house
guma'

rat
chå'ka

cloud
mapagåhes

whale
bayena

starfish
puti'on tåsi

bulldozer
butdosa'

flip flops
yori'

bicycle
bisikleta

book
lepblo

baby bottle
boteyan neni

policeman
pulisia

submarine
båtkon påpa' tåsi

shark
halu'u

tree
trongko

flag
bandera

cat
katu

banana
aga'

Santa claus
Santa klos

money
salape'

plane
batkon airi

firetruck
tråk guafi

toilet bowl
sagan tuminani'

ant
otdot

hat
tuhung

newspaper
gaseta

bus
bås

table
lamasa

heart
korason

box
kahita

lunch bag
saguan tengguang

purse
balakbak

tire
taiha'

coin
sinsiyu

shoe
sapåtos

notepad
lepblon manggi'

fly
lålu

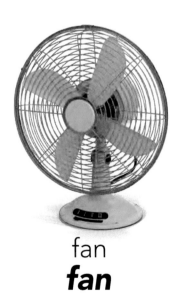

fan
fan

bag
butsiyu

ice cream
ais krim

waste basket
sagan basula

mosquito
ñåmu

rock
åcho'

helicopter
helikåpta

doctor
dokto

couch
sagan matå'chong

glass
båsun mamafak

jet ski
yetski

fork
tenidot

star
puti'on

wagon
karetan patgon

baby shoes
sapåtos neni

fruit
fruta

pineapple
piña

bread basket
basket pån

bell
kampåna

firewood
håyu

paper plane
påpit batkon airi

sun
åtdao

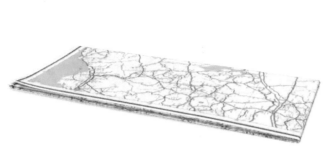

map
måpa

snail
akaleha'

flowers
china'lik

needle
hagua

clock
rilos

boat
boti

watering can
hareran hanom

bed
kåtri

spoon
kuchåla

turtle
hagan

stick
håyu

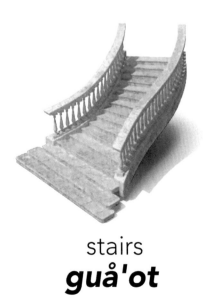

stairs
guå'ot

laptop
laptåp

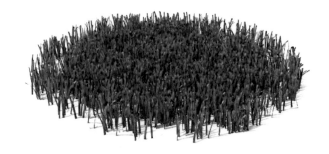

grass
chå'guan

plate
plåtu

teddy bear
teddi beir

paint
pintura

pen
pluma

horse
kabåyu

pool
sagan umo'mak

umbrella
påyu

hammer
mattiyu

ladder
gua'ot

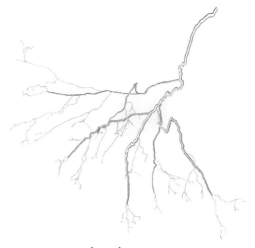

lightning
lamlam

crayons
kre'on

cookie
kukis

hot air balloon
batkon airen abubu

scissors
tieras

egg
chåda'

bird
paluma

kite
papaloti

baby stroller
karetan neni

snake
kolepbla

rope
tåli

moon
pulan

chair
siya

elephant
elifanti

clam
hima

cross
kilu'us

fire hydrant
hos guafi

cement block
åcho' simentu

soap
håbun mama'gåsi

frog
kairo'

light switch
fafanila'

popsicle
påpsiko'

milk carton
katton lechi

chocolate candy
kandin chikolåti

corn
korn

coffee beans
simiyan kafe

drawer
kåhun

baby food
na' neni

computer
komputa

diver
ñañangu

ring
aniyu

hair brush
brås gapotulu

judge
hues

soldier
mimimu

shirt
franela

rooster
gayu

sunglasses
anti'os somnak

candy
kandi

meat
katni

Earth
Tano'

television
telebision

dining table
lamasan chumochu

saw
chåchak

mirror
espehus

plant
tinanom

shovel
påla

washer
makinan mama'gåsi

lawn mower
lonmowa

crib
kuna

flash light
kandit

picture frame
sagan litråtu

towel
tu'åya

knives
se'si'

refrigerator
ais bak

gas pump
bomban gas

paper towel
tu'åyan papit

lamp shade
tampin kandit

pillow
alunan

sugar
asukat

barbecue grill
sagan manunu

chopping board
famikåyan

light bulb
kandit

trash truck
tråk basula

baseball mit
glåf bola

dog bowl
plåtun ga'lågu

book shelf
sagan lepblo

food container
sagan nengkanno'

carpet
atfombra

sea horse
kabåyun tåsi

can
låta

neck tie
kutbåta

hospital
espitåt

comb
paini

false teeth
nifin timagåhit

camera
litratu

bee
abeha

guitar
gitåla

jellyfish
abubon papago'

stingray
fanihin tåsi

lobster
mahongang

candle
dångis

octopus
gamson

office
ofisina

curtain
kuttina

measuring tape
tep midida

green beans
abuchuelas

onion
siboyas

deer
binådu

letter mail
katta

hammerhead shark
halu'u

diamond
diamonti

roses
flores rosa

cockroach
kukuråcha

potato
batåtas

rocking chair
siyan chukan

cleaver
machettin mata'dot

anchor
angkla

eggplant
biringenas

diapers
pañåles

grapes
ubas

paper clip
go'tin papit

dolphin
tuninus

scorpion
ñufo'

music
dandan

door
potta

spider
sanyeye'

piano
pianu

swing
amåka

bank
bånku

See other interesting titles from the Gerard Aflague Collection

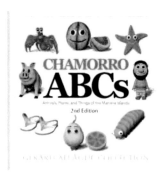
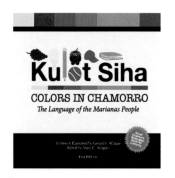

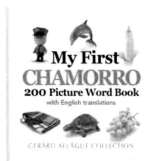
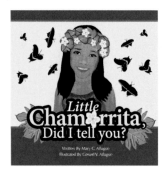

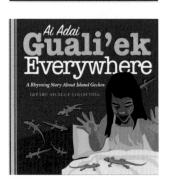

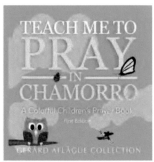

Buy titles on GerardAflagueCollection.com, Amazon.com, and eBay.com

 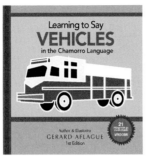   

About the Editor

Mary Aflague was born and raised on the beautiful island of Guam. Now residing in Colorado, she still manages to enjoy the outdoors and sunshine. She is a career educator in the Denver Public School district instilling in her students, the joy and power of being life-long readers and learners. Her interests include writing and editing children's books, reading, yoga, art, traveling, and Pacific Island dance.

About the Author and Designer

Gerard Aflague is a long-time Guam native, now residing in Colorado. He enjoys illustrating and publishing cultural books that inspire, educate, and entertain. In addition to self-publishing books, he researches and writes reports informing Congress about information technology issues in the Federal government. He is a passionate product designer, inventor, and entrepreneur. He designs educational resources that are in thousands of homes and classrooms in over a dozen countries including the United States, Canada, the Netherlands, Germany, France, Australia, and New Zealand. When he finds free time in his busy schedule, he spends it with family traveling, enjoying good food, and reading a good book.

The Gerard Aflague Collection has 100+ books published to date. Many titles are bilingual learning fundamentals for children in a variety of languages including English, Chamorro, Hawaiian, Tongan, Samoan, Spanish, Tagalog, Vietnamese, Afrikaans, Amerhic, Palauan, Chuukese, Yapese, and Korean, among others.

Aflague has sold over 8,000 books to date distributed across the world, and more unique titles are being designed and published monthly offering unique reading resources online. The collection also offers 750 home, office, and auto products sold on the GerardAflagueCollection.com.

Made in the USA
Columbia, SC
23 February 2019